MW01258199

EMOTIONAL ADDICTION –

A Bitter Sweet Truth

by

Kathie Mathis, Psy.D

1

FOREWORD

I am honored to be asked by Dr. Kathie Mathis to introduce this insightful, practical and personal guide to recognize, handle and heal from personal addiction. Most of us, if not all, have experienced some form of addition in their lives, in terms of alcohol, drugs, nicotine, food, and many other forms that if not treated properly, and because we are all connected, it can have serious adverse impact on people's lives. There are many reasons why we become addicted to one of more of these forms and in most cases the source of the problem can be traced back to what we have experienced or how we feel about something that cause us to become addicts. Of all the forms, living in an abused relationship, physical and/or emotional, has the greatest impact because it touches the core of our being and it requires special attention to heal from such horrible experiences. Dr. Mathis has created a wonderful guide to assist us in understanding the various forms of addiction, recognizing how emotional imbalances in personal relationships can hook us into thinking that things are not that bad, when instead could lead to serious health issues if we don't break free.

Dr. Mathis' passion in assisting domestic violence victims to "break free" from a horrific life transcends our time. Having experienced an unhealthy life from living in toxic relationships, Dr. Mathis has tapped into her personal growth and wisdom she has gained over the years to share her life with those who seem stuck and not able to see the light at the end of the dark tunnel. Over the past twenty years, Dr. Mathis has dedicated her life as a state and national advocate who meets with legislators in Washington D.C. and California, as well as with California's Supreme Court Justice and Judicial Council, promoting legislation and safety measures for abused children and women. Dr. Mathis has traveled across country speaking and training nonprofits, churches, colleges, teachers, businesses and county employees; she has appeared on many television programs and hosted a television program "Real People Real Problems, Real Solutions" which offers solutions to problems with relationships, domestic abuse, child abuse and teen issues; among her many other accomplishments, Dr. Mathis was invited to have lunch with President Bush in March 2008 and receive the Congressional Medal of Merit but was not able to attend the luncheon because it conflict with a previously scheduled meeting with a major Airline in finalizing a "Fly Home" program for domestic violence victims.

Even with all this National recognition, Dr. Mathis is crystal clear on her intention to help each victim to overcome hurts and pains and restore to a healthier and more satisfying life. I remember one time when I was asked to be a guest speaker at one of Dr. Mathis' workshop programs and waited in the wings to take the stage, I was moved by the discussion and the writing on the whiteboard. Dr. Mathis had written a list of signs of someone who has probably been raised in an abused family. Even though I was never physical abused as a child, I knew that there was physical abuse in my family but I never thought of myself as a victim. I thought I was the strong one who became the caretaker in assisting others to break free from the abuse but never thought that those experiences had impacted my life. Upon reflection and after listening to Dr. Mathis that day, I realized that my emotional scars were deep and everything made sense why it has taken me many years to break free from it. It has been said many times before by others that nothing is truly learned until it is realized. Thank you Dr. Mathis for making me realize this and for all the inspiring work that you do each day. You are one-of-a-kind and this world is a better place because of you.

Love,
Costantino Delli
www.cosdelli.com

INTRODUCTION

'Life is not the way it's supposed to be. It's the way it is. The way you cope with it is what makes the difference.'

One of the central issues in our lives is to reconcile the pleasures of intellectual thought and scientific thought with the sense of purpose and fulfillment that a spiritual life provides. If we examine research and study on genetic material in organisms as well as religious beliefs, we can come to some conclusions that help us make sense of some of the traumas and life experiences we have.

This book is about explaining and breaking an emotional addiction that develops from trauma and experiences we have. The choices we made helped create the addictions but can be changed to help us lead better lives. Scientific and spiritual research is discussed for clarity on emotional addiction and can have both thought. But this book is not only about research but also about experiences the author has had, as well as experiences clients shared on their own journey to having happier and healthier lives.

In the book "The God Gene" there is fascinating data which includes tests done on meditating Buddhist monks who relinquish ordinary thought processes in favor of a state of loss – loss of the sense of time and space, of cause and effect of selfhood. "As Buddhists meditate, they consciously attempt to clear their minds…they send signals through the thalamus to the cortex, the seat of the will." They divert energy from "core" consciousness into "secondary or higher consciousness."

Evangelicals reject the idea that faith might be reduced to chemical reactions in the brain and Humanists refuse to accept that religious belief is inherent in people's makeup.

The author is of the belief that it is both of these, chemical reactions in the brain as well as inherent in people's makeup. Many scientists, including Dean H. Hamer, have studied spirituality. In "The God Gene: How Faith is Hardwired Into Our Genes" Hamer found that the brain chemicals associated with anxiety and other emotions, including joy and sadness, appeared to be in play in the deep meditative states of Zen practitioners and the prayerful repose of Roman Catholic nuns, as well as mystical trances brought on by users of peyote and other mind-altering drugs. He stated, "Our genes can predispose us to believe. But they don't tell us what to believe in." Choice is the key.

What is emotion? There are many different scientific thoughts about what an emotion is or isn't. Emotion is one of the most controversial topics in psychology, a source of intense discussion and disagreement from the earliest philosophers to thinkers of today. Most agree that emotion has "components" made up of physiological and psychological factors and include emotion faces, emotion elicitors, and emotion neural processes. A broad consensus has emerged on what we might call adequacy conditions on any theory of emotion. An acceptable philosophical theory of emotions should be able to account at least for the following nine characteristics. All the recent and current accounts of emotion discussed here have something to say about most of them, and some have had something to say about all.

- emotions are typically conscious phenomena;
- yet they typically involve more pervasive bodily manifestations than other conscious states;
- they vary along a number of dimensions: intensity, valence, type and range of intentional objects, etc.
- they are reputed to be antagonists of rationality;
- also they play an indispensable role in determining the quality of life;
- they contribute crucially to defining our ends and priorities;
- they play a crucial role in the regulation of social life;

- they protect us from an excessively slavish devotion to narrow conceptions of rationality;
- they have a central place in moral education and the moral life.

The exploration of questions raised by these nine characteristics is a thriving ongoing collaborative project in the theory of emotions, in which philosophy will continue both to inform and to draw on a wide range of philosophical expertise as well as the parallel explorations of other branches of cognitive science. (Emotions by unknown author).

At the core of common sense approaches to emotion is the one that people have in mind when talking about human emotions – the feeling component or the passion or sensation of emotion. Another obvious component is the set of behaviors that may be performed and observed in conjunction with an emotion.

Whatever your philosophy on what makes an emotion – the hope is that you find your way to believe that you can be a fulfilled person and that emotional addiction can be broken through different modalities including, choice, counseling, life experience, faith, meditation, and scientific methods. This book is one small way that can help you. Change is work but something so worth the effort – and it begins with a "spark."

PREFACE

We have been conditioned into believing things about ourselves from the time we were small. Some of us were shown by parents who had poor parenting skills that we were not smart enough, good enough, important enough, lovable enough; just not "enough" of anything to be valued by them. Our very sense of who we were is attacked before we even formed a sense of who we were or had the opportunity to form that sense of who we are. We learned and experienced heartbreak at an early age. So why wouldn't we be screwed up as an adult?

Our lives needed to begin with the knowledge that our fathers cherished us and that our mothers loved us and both of them wanted us and at least, wanted to spend some time with us. The job of making us feel good, enjoyed, treasured and safe as well as "enough" seems an overwhelming chore to adults who have abuse, addictions, and other issues that keep them from this very important duty and responsibility. So our hearts and souls have empty spaces and we ache to be treasured, honored, cherished, and loved and most of all "enough."

Deep within every human being lies the true spirit essence of our being, an energy or spark that gives us all our sameness and connection. Recent research has shown that in all blue-eyed individuals there is something in the eye gene that is "exactly" the same in all blue-eyed individuals showing that all blue-eyed humans are related. Scientists will probably find the same in all brown-eyed humans. What make us different are our experiences - experiences that we have throughout our lives and those that are genetically passed on to us by our ancestors. Each moment we experience life will ignite the spark within us or cover it up. The good news is that no matter what we experience with drugs, abuse, food, relationships and "life events," we will always have a bit of that "spark" waiting to re-ignite. Love, compassion, honoring, kindness, caring and nurturing will make it glow, lighting up the coldest and loneliest places in our heart and spirit.

Here is the reason I wrote this book: to let you know that the healing of your heart is available and that my desire is to help you on your journey to find that healing. To help you overcome hurts and pains and to release emotional addiction created by those experiences, restoring your life to a healthier level so you can flourish and become happier - that is my passion.

So how does one improve emotional health? First, take time to recognize and understand why you are having certain emotions. Being able to sort them out helps identify causes of sadness, stress and anxiety in your life and helps you to manage your emotional health.

Express your feelings appropriately and don't stuff them down inside. It's okay to let your family know when something is bothering you, but keep in mind that they may not be able to help you deal with those feelings. In this case, ask someone trained to help you such as a counselor, doctor, religious advisor, or therapist for advice and support. This will improve your coping abilities as well as your emotional health.

Try not to obsess about problems but live a balanced life. Deal with negative feelings, but try to focus on the positive things in life as well. Ways to deal with balance are given in this book so that you can find balance of mind, body and soul. Having good health is important to emotional health and good decision-making.

This especially applies to women - for this book is for and about women and conditions often befalling women. However, men will find useful information within its pages as well which can be applied to their emotional addictions.

CHAPTER ONE

Relational Women

Most women are relationally based. From the time we are small, we develop relationships with other girls, our dolls, our pets and especially our mothers and fathers. Our sense of self and how we see ourselves as grown women is shaped by our early relationships as little girls. Our mothers teach us what it means to be a woman and our fathers teach us the value we have as a woman. Our relationship with others teach us what the world thinks of us.

For centuries women have lived with relational fellowship with other women. We gathered and gossiped at the river as we did laundry. We talked to each other over fences while we hung our laundry on the clothesline to dry. We met at wells as we filled our water jugs and discussed the politics of the day. When young women were in accompaniment of their mother or older sister, information on what it means to be a woman and what femininity is, was passed along naturally. It was a means of "passage" where women gathered information about the men in the community, business in the community, religion in the community and the culture in which they were to live. These times were stamped into women's relationship memory book – their brain.

In today's world most of us don't go to the well to draw water, or to the river to wash our clothes (however in some countries these practices still take place). Most of us have clothes dryers, washing machines, running water in our houses, and other modern conveniences. When we meet women it is in church, at the PTA, at committee meetings, or at Mommy and Me classes. Agenda's, rigid time constrictions set activities, deadlines, and other modern problems like grid lock, two jobs, and more, keep us from experiencing the "relational" learning, socializing, and passage turning from little girls into women. We watch and learn from our mothers, grandmothers and other adult women in our lives if they have the time to be relational with us but mostly we learn from television and the movies.

Mothers and fathers need to be present, need to enjoy, and to love and hug lavishly. They need to be tender with their children's souls and emotions, to have close and caring relationships with them.

Studies have shown that women who have reported having close and caring relationships with their fathers and mothers suffer less eating disorders, depression, addictions, illness and anxieties. They had a "strong sense of personal identity and positive self esteem." (Margo Maine, Father Hunger).

"There can be no knowledge without emotion. We may be aware of a truth, yet until we have felt its force, it is not ours. To the cognition of the brain must be added the experience of the soul."
Arnold Bennett (1867-1931)

My mother and I loved spending time together talking about everything. We were extremely close as mothers and daughters go and I was always happy when we got to spend time together. I can remember from the time I was a little girl that her love was never withheld, never conditional, or selfish. Her love and emotional support encouraged me to flourish throughout my life, to have positive attitude, and to know no matter what came my way, I could face the challenges before me. She told me, "Kathie, always remember that one can always cry and be depressed. That is easy to do when things go wrong in one's life. But to keep positive, look for solutions, and act on those solutions, takes strength, courage, and resilience. You have all of those. Always remember you come from good "stock" and we don't believe in giving up."

I have had very few health problems over my life, which I attribute to her love, emotional support, and advice to be positive, find solutions to problems. Even when I felt weak and scared, I had known I had courage because I came from "good stock" and could make it through anything. Thanks Mom.

CHAPTER TWO

Trauma Bonding/Love Confusion

Those of us who did not have loving, caring, and emotionally and physically present parents as we were growing up were born just like everyone else, with this "spark" in our soul but also with early experiences that left us hurting. Our parents brought into our early lives deprivation of "connection" to them in the form of inconsistent love (trauma bonding), deprivation of love, and everything in between. Their gift to us was their guilt's, fears, hang-ups, abuse, addictions and genetic problems. And we took it all in, absorbed it like a sponge, and made decisions about ourselves like we were not valued because we were told to "shut up," "leave me alone," "you're an idiot like your mother," or "like your father" and so on. We made oaths that we would not be like our mothers or fathers as we dreamed of escaping and finding someone or something to love us and give us back the "spark" that was slowly being smothered in our lives. So we began seeking those things to fill our lives that will fill us up and make the "spark" return. And the choices we make were not always the ones with positive outcomes.

The level of bonding between a parent and child is extremely important to the well-being and self-esteem of a child and its emotional addiction. Systematic abuse – particularly of a kind that involves cycles of intermittent fear and kindness – can lead to the formation of unusually strong but unhealthy bonds and can foster the victim's development of potent dependence on the abuser (Dutton, 1995; James, 1994; Dutton & Painter, 1993; Herman, 1992).

"A few central dynamics of traumatic bonding should be highlighted. First, one of the effects of abuse is to create a potent longing in the victim for kindness and understanding, and for relief from the fear or terror experienced (Dutton & Painter, 1993). A person who is able to provide soothing treatment at the right moment will tend to be perceived by the victim as a rescuer, and so to be looked upon with gratitude. In traumatic bonding, the person who brings the soothing relief is the same one who perpetrated the abuse.

Following an incident of abuse, for example, an abuser may apologize for what happened, express concern for how the victim is feeling, and speak in a calm and warm tone. The typical response in victims of abuse is to feel thankful for the kindness, to be eager to forgive, and to form a belief that the abuser actually cares deeply for him or her. Once this cycle has been repeated a number of times, the victim may come to feel grateful to the abuser for just stopping the abuse each time, even if no real kindness or attentiveness follows. This has been demonstrated to be a normal response to abuse related trauma in males and in females (Herman, 1992) rather than a masochistic trait in females as was assumed previously, and the intermittency of the abuse has been demonstrated to be a critical reason for the strength of trauma bonds (Dutton & Painter, 1993) (Bancroft & Silverman, 2002)."

Children and adults can become bonded to protect their abusers. They can gradually become "love confused" just like the abuser. Because the "loving behavior" follows so closely the "trauma" behavior, the two become psychologically and emotionally linked in the victim's brain (Dutton & Painter, 1993).

Traumatic bonding leads the child to become increasingly focused "on the needs, wants, and emotional state of the abusive adult (which)….causes the child to lose focus on developing his or her abilities or engaging with the world (Whitten, 1994, p.35).

Factors that can help re-ignite the inner spark of a young person are the development of talents, interests, and relationships with trustworthy adults. When adults empower a child with words like, "you are special," or "you are so smart" or "you make me so proud" then children's inner spark is ignited into limitless possibilities. Choices in letting go of self-blame, negative influences and messages, creating strengths in peer relationships with positive influences, help to create nurturing and resilience while developing personal strengths and reducing trauma bonding.

CHAPTER THREE

The Brain – What we don't see!

"Someday, after we have mastered the winds, the waves, the tides and gravity, we shall harness for God the energies of love. Then, for the second time in the history of the world, man will have discovered fire."
Teilhard de Chardin

Studies have shown that 75% of the information our brains take in during a day is negative information and only 25% is positive information. The horrors that abusive mothers and fathers have on young lives and the wounds imprinted in young brains goes to the very core of our souls. It breaks hearts, heaps shame, and creates feelings of unworthiness, un-love-ableness, minimization of self, valueless. Along with other negative experiences and messages, it makes us emotionally ill as well as physically ill. It strips us of our natural spirit self and leaves us sick, broken, empty, and damaged to the point that we don't know who we are and what we want.

But some of what we experience doesn't manifest itself in this manner and remains unseen and is equally, if not more, damaging. If we don't understand or know about emotional shame then how can we trust it? If we haven't acknowledged our fears, how can we overcome them? If our lives are unmanageable and out of control, and we don't stop to take care of it and keep stuffing more into it hoping no one notices – how can we expect our relationships with our partners, children, friends, family, bosses – and most importantly ourselves, to be fulfilling?

Our hearts desire is to be loved and to be amazing to our partner. We want to be "enough" - not "too much" or "too controlling" or too critical, over bearing, aggressive, sexual, overweight, loud, thin and so on....! We want to be "enough" yet outside messages tell us we are to be more – to be "perfect" and so we wear our masks and hide our true spirit and self. Our emotional addiction comes to be our friend and gives us feelings of "perfectness" or "wholeness" or "enough."

Our body uses combinations of special chemicals to produce each of the different emotions. Do you know that there is a certain chemical combination for happiness, and sadness, and anger, and victimization, and any other emotion that you can think of?

Throughout the years, people develop an addiction to the different chemicals of different emotions. The point is the more people feel a certain emotion, the more addicted to that emotion they become. For example, if you get angry on a consistent basis, you develop an emotional addiction to the anger chemicals. If you play a victim and cry "why" long enough, you habituate that way of being and develop an emotional addiction to those specific chemicals. As each of the cells divides, the new cells that are created need more and more of those specific chemicals in order to get the same stimulation as the old cell.

So how does this all connect with the law of attraction? Our usual emotional state attracts to us more of that emotional state. So one can see that if addicted to specific emotional states, we have to undo the habitual addiction to those negative emotional states and develop new behaviors and habits for the positive emotional chemicals. Thus, one will often act in particular ways just to get the fix of one's emotional addiction. The real difficulty for many people is to get past emotional addictions and develop more productive and positive emotional addictions. One will need to practice new behaviors in order to develop new habits and therefore new emotional and positive emotions. This is very difficult the first time; nevertheless, with enough practice it becomes easy to stay happy because of your addiction to that particular positive emotional condition. The point is - the more you practice those positive emotions - the easier it gets over time because your body will naturally develop an addiction for those emotional chemicals and attract situations and people to you in order to maintain that emotional addiction. Practice positive emotions, and eventually the universe will throw situations and people at you in order to maintain that emotional addiction. Studies sow that it takes approximately 22 - 27 days to change a behavior when repeated several times daily.

You can't look to others for validation of your inner spirit and soul. No one can tell you who you are as a woman, a man, a person. And no one can give you a verdict on who you are even though they may want to be your judge and jury. They are not reliable, honest, and safe sources. But you can validate who you are. You can break emotional addiction and honor your personhood. So let's look at how to begin this more fully.

Dean Hamer, author of "The God Gene" began looking in 1998, when he was conducting a survey on smoking and addiction for the National Cancer Institute. As part of his study, he recruited over 1,000 women and men who agreed to take a standardized, 240 question personality test called the Temperament and Character Inventory (TCI). Among the traits the TCI measures is one known as self-transcendence, which consists of three other traits: self-forgetfulness (the ability to get entirely lost in an experience); transpersonal identification (feeling connectedness to a larger universe); and mysticism (openness to things not literally provable). Put these all together and science comes as close as it can to measuring what it feels like to be spiritual.

"This allows us to have the kind of experience described as religious ecstasy," says Robert Cloninger, Washington University psychiatrist and designer of the transcendence portion of the TCI.

Hamer decided to use the data he gathered in the smoking survey to conduct a little spirituality study on the side. He first ranked the participants among Cloninger's self-transcendence scale placing them on a continuum from least to most spiritually inclined. Then he studied their genes to see if he could find the DNA responsible for the differences. No easy task with 35,000 genes consisting of 3.2 billion chemical bases. So to narrow the field, Hamer confined his work to nine specific genes known to play major roles in production of monoamines – brain chemicals, including serotonin, norephinephrine and dopamine that regulate such fundamental functions as mood and motor control. It's monoamines that are carefully manipulated by Prozac and other antidepressants.

Studying the nine candidate genes in DNA samples provided by the study subjects, Hamer hit the genetic markers. A variation in a gene known as vmal2 – for vesicular monoamine transporter – seemed to be directly related to how the volunteers scored on the self-transcendence test. Those with the nucleic acid cytosine in one particular spot on the gene ranked higher than those with the nucleic acid adenine in the same spot. "A single change in the single base in the middle of the gene seemed directly related to the ability to feel self-transcendence," Hamer stated. Merely having that feeling did not mean those people would take the next step and translate their transcendence into a belief in – or even a quest for – God, but they seemed likelier to do so.

Hamer was careful to point out that the gene he found is by no means the only one that affects spirituality. Even minor human traits can be governed by the interplay of many genes. A complex belief possibly could involve hundreds, if not more, genes.

Hamer stressed that while he may have located a genetic root for spirituality that it is not the same as a genetic root for religion. Spirituality is a feeling or state of mind; religion is they way that states gets manifested. Understanding a bit of the emotional connection many have to their religion is now better understood. Hamer puts it this way, "Spirituality is intensely personal; religion is institutional."

Neuroscientist Andrew Newberg of the University of Pennsylvania School of Medicine researched how spirituality plays out in the brain. He used several types of imaging systems to watch brains of subjects as they meditate or pray. By measuring blood flow, he determines which regions are responsible for the feelings the volunteers experienced. The deeper the subjects descended into meditation or prayer, the more active the frontal lobe and the limbic system became. The frontal lobe is the seat of concentration and attention. The limbic system is where our powerful feelings, including rapture, are processed. More revealing is this fact: at the same time these regions flash to life, another important region in the back of the brain – the parietal lobe – goes dim. It's this lobe that orients the individual in time and space. Take it off-line and the boundaries of the self fall away creating a feeling of being one with the universe. When you combine that with what is going on in the other two lobes, you can have a profound spiritual experience.

Avise wrote in the book "The Genetic Gods" that genes have special powers over human lives and affairs. The genetic material in organisms alive today traces back generation to generation through an unbroken chain of descent (with modifications) from ancestral molecules that have copied and replaced themselves ever since the origin of life on earth, about 4 billion years ago."

Hamer stated that more research has to be done to determine more gene responsibilities in humans." Women seem to score higher than men on transcendence tests and he believed this was true because women are more attuned to their emotional connections.

Emotional addiction then comes from genetics, ancestry, behaviors and attitudes, and connections or lack of to our spirituality. Emotional addiction is the condition of being habitually or compulsively occupied with or involved in something.

A woman, I will call her Karen, came to me for help. She was married to a man for 13 years who abused her physically and verbally. She came in crying one afternoon stating she had discovered that despite everything she had experienced from him, she loved him and wanted me to help her not want him. Karen was obviously crushed and angry at the same time. She was emotionally devastated by the betrayal of his love and didn't know what to do except show her anger. She wanted me to help her figure out a way to help her so she could stay and be safe at the same time.

Karen's emotional addiction to her husband kept her from overcoming her denial of his behaviors and attitudes in the relationship and breaking her trust. It also kept her from allowing herself to receive her recovery because she stayed in her "hope" that he would change even though he was doing nothing to change except make her promises to do so. She stayed with him because of her emotional addiction as well as her "learned helplessness" and because of his "promises" and manipulative deeds, which she desperately wanted to believe and have – all of which served a purpose for them both. The last time I saw Karen she stated that she would never trust him, but she would stay with him no matter what.

CHAPTER FOUR

The Awakening!

In the movie "Minority Report,' Tom Cruise plays a police chief who runs a pre-crime program in the year 2020. His character uses three "pre-cogs" or pre-cognition individuals who are wired up to electrodes, floating in a watery bath, who send "messages" and pictures to a screen of what events they see before the events happen. Tom and his team then go and stop the crime before it happens.

In "What the Bleep Do We Know" the neurobiologists talk about the brain and that the brain imprints what the eyes see but that the eyes see more than what the brain can imprint. The brain processes 400 billion bits of information a second yet it process's only 2000 of those bits of information, revealing that we don't see everything because the brain can't process everything the eyes see. We only see what we think is possible and because we are conditioned to see and believe things, the brain follow along with that conditioning. Again, our eyes see more than what the brain can project.

There is a story told in "What The Bleep Do We Know" about Columbus and the Native American Indians. It is told that when the Native Americans saw Columbus and his ships out in the harbor that they did not see them at first because they had no knowledge of what ships were. So to them there was nothing there. But a Shaman saw ripples on the water and wondered what created them and began to investigate. For several days he watched the water until he discovered the source - he saw the ships. He went to the native Indians and told them what he had seen. They believed him because he was a Shaman, and when they looked out into the harbor, they saw the ships as well. They could not process something they did not believe in or had knowledge of but when someone they believed in told them about the ships, they saw because their perceptions changed.

Abused victims don't always believe in the beginning of the abusive relationship, that they are experiencing abuse because they have no knowledge of what abuse is (unless they grew up in a home where abuse was experienced). They continue in the relationship despite others telling them they might be in trouble. They don't believe until they are emotionally addicted, trauma bonded, isolated and in full fear for themselves and their children if they have children. Our brains need to "see" and process what our experiences are visually and emotionally.

The brain looks like a thunderstorm when producing a thought. Electricity comes down from one part to another. Emotion and ideas are the same – neurons fire and brain remembers what the eyes see. We connect events to a picture and react to it based on the emotional response we have attached to it.

Emotions are holographic reactions to our experiences. There are chemicals for every emotional state we experience. The hypothalamus creates peptides which it sends out to thousands of receptors on one cell. They attach and signal what goes into our cells (What the bleep do I Know). We become addicted to an emotional state and stay addicted unless we change our attachments, emotions, and beliefs about things.

We are emotions and emotions are we. Emotions enrich our experience but our addictions to these emotions are the problem because they create bio-chemical addictions. When you think of all of your experiences with the emotions you have attached to them - from the brain going down to the very cells of your body - no wonder it is hard to leave abusive relationships, people, food, and sex. No wonder it is hard to overcome drug and alcohol addictions, food addictions, gambling addictions and more. Not only is the recovery process changing attitudes and beliefs, it is also receiving and applying educational information, which creates a bio-chemical addiction recovery on both physical and spiritual levels.

"When the clarity of compassion illuminates our vision, we can visualize healing that goes deeper than physical care....We recognize that this could be an opportunity for tragedy to be transformed into celebration so that the power of God may be seen at work in him and her."

Author Unknown

CHAPTER FIVE

WANT

We can know some of our future by looking at our past. We learn from our past so that we don't repeat negative things that have occurred in our lives that we don't want to take into our future. We know that if we don't exercise, we won't be as healthy as we could be and disease could set in. We know that if we drink too much alcohol, we will become drunk; we know that if we kill another human being, society's rules state we will go to jail and possibly prison. There are lots of books that give us information on what our future can be like and ways to live better and happier lives such as the Koran, Bible, Tora, Ghandi's writings, Buddha's writings, and so forth.

But to honor who we are means that first of all must "want" to honor ourselves. From the time we are small, the inner urging or voice has told us about ourselves. It has made us aware of the need to eat, sleep, wake up, smile, laugh, talk, and feel. But as children, we weren't able to totally understand this inner voice fully. It sometimes gave us mixed messages we had to decipher and make sense of. For some of us, this process has taken years.

Now please don't misunderstand this next statement shared with you regarding mixed messages and our trying to make sense of things that were and are non-decipherable – "GET OVER IT!" Don't go around whining, bragging, or wearing things negative like a badge of honor. Get off the "Pity Pot" and WANT to move forward and get moving that direction. Not to be un-sympathetic totally, there are certain things that we definitely need to get extra help with by talking with a mental health professional. But most of us hang on to things that we shouldn't. Many of us want to justify our experience by hanging onto something we could let go of, and repeat again and again, the facts of that experience. We proudly wear our "this happened to me" buttons and sit in support groups meant to help us overcome the experience, but instead we use as an arena for "my story is worse than your story," and never get the benefits that we were meant to get.

In my experience in working with domestic violence victims, I have seen this happen over and over as a new woman comes into the support group for recovery from abuse. They are allowed, as a new member, to tell their experience of trauma so that they immediately get support, love, and encouragement from the group along with the healing effects of getting the story "out" and releasing the trauma. Ugly things happen to some of us and we need to get the help necessary. But we also need to keep moving through life at the same time we are healing. We haven't always been told the truth by family and friends - we haven't always had the loving partner in our lives we were meant to have. We have been betrayed by those we trusted and some of us have had our innocence lost much to early in our lives. These things should not happen to anyone – ever! But in our world, the reality is there are many sick individuals who do harm. But we can't give them the power over our lives for the rest of our lives by hanging on to the "my story is worse than your story" mentality and move into "wanting" and "awareness" of healing, healthiness and wholeness. We are in charge of our lives and therefore we define our lives and not the perpetrator or the trauma the perpetrator has inflicted on us.

We all have experienced terrible traumas in our lives and we all can speak from experience on this topic. We must get over the emotional addiction we have to the trauma and its story. We need to do more with our lives than stay in victim-hood and trauma bonding relationships. We don't need to hang on to the non-truths we've been told and believed, and must let things go so we can free up space to replace those non-truths with truths. We can replace those old messages, emotional addiction pathways from our brains to our cells with new messages and pathways, which benefit us. How can we be "aware" of real needs and truths when we are cluttering our minds with negatives given to us by others?

If you add the negative input we create ourselves to what we receive from others, you then have so much clutter that the brain is overloaded from it. We must allow the 2000 bits of information the brain receives a second to process healthy things only.

THE BRAIN

```
                              /
   10 % Conscious      /
                           / -------Critical Area
                         /
                       /      90% Subconscious
```

The information that comes into the conscious part of our brain is separated from the subconscious part of our brain by what is called the "critical area." We need to get new information that we want to replace old information from the conscious to the subconscious area of our brain where information is stored and where our emotions to a situation come from. There are different methods to make this process happen which include the following:

Affirmations: assertion statement. The act of affirming or asserting or stating something

Journaling: a ledger or book in which something is recorded or written

Meditation: continuous and profound contemplation or musing on a subject or series of subjects of a deep or abstruse nature

Visualizing: a mental image that is similar to a visual perception

Endless Tape: listening to your voice recording affirmations and positive messages on a tape that continues without stopping while you are sleeping

Alpha State: Research has found that the ideal state for learning is when the brain is in a relaxed, but aware state. So when we say relaxed, we do not mean asleep. We mean relaxed, focused and aware. At this point the brainwaves run at about 8 to 12 cycles per seconds or hertz. This is called the **alpha state**.

CHAPTER SIX

"Searching"

Now that the knowledge of "wanting" has been explained for recovery of emotional addiction and healthy living, we move into the next step of "searching" and looking at options, knowledge and experience as considerations.

The definition of "search" in Webster's dictionary is: "to look through in trying to find something." "Critical examination." "Seek, Probe."

As a result of the wounds we received growing up (which caused the bio-chemicals to be released from the brain to the cells leaving us with emotions to situations that developed into emotional addiction), we come to believe that part of us, if not all of us, is marred. If we stay in this shame it cripples us deep within our souls. This soul shame can make us crippled enough to not want to search. This shame makes us feel – no, believe – that if others really knew us they would run away in horror if not disgust and disdain. This shame-based belief grips our souls and holds us down, ever ready to spotlight our shortcomings, abuse, and addictions and judge us no matter what has affected us. We know we aren't "enough" and we lack! Shame tells us we are unworthy, broken, bad, despairing, and beyond repair; that we deserve the pain we know. So we must hide and wear masks that please others so we won't be alone. We hide under addictions, isolation, religion, eating disorders, body piercing, body cutting, tattoos and other things. We put out our "Do Not Disturb" sign and hide, hide, hide. We place the spotlight on this sign so no one "enters" our "space" and hurt us further by finding out what we are really like or adding to our own disgust with ourselves.

But just the opposite of hiding is what we need to do. In the game of hide and seek, one hides and another seeks. Seeking and "searching" to change our emotional addiction and become the person we are intended to be is another building block to stopping our addiction. We "seek" and "probe" through means of therapy, counseling, spiritual enrichment and healing, forgiveness, medication or whatever we need as we take our journey of living fully. One thing we do know is that we are miserable in our state of emotional addiction and we need to search out ways to change it.

To take the next step on this journey to gain peace and personal power, we must go through a place of discomfort and probing of our lives. We must go into ourselves, to our very souls and heart, and we want to run in the opposite direction. It is hard to tell ourselves that we must "feel" and re-experience some trauma's to over come them. We must work on self when it is easier to "blame" or "justify" or "sit on the pity pot" and complain about how bad we have it or had it. It is simpler to take a drug, to eat, to continue being comfortable in our pain and so we stay there. But you must take this journey of searching because you are worth the rewards of a new state of belief about yourself. You are in charge of your future and you alone must make this effort to take the action that is necessary and to experience "healthy selfishness" and set boundaries, have goals, cry about trauma's if we haven't, and let others opinion's, messages, and expressions become non-important.

Take a moment here and ask yourself, "Am I worth the effort? Are the messages of hurt that I have received really something I need to continue to hold? What does it serve me to hold on to them and what would it serve me to let them go?" When one chooses to let something go then the blank spot left needs to be filled with more self-love things.

In the movie "As Good As It Gets" the character played by Jack Nicholson says to Helen Hunts character, "You make me want to be a better man." He looked to her and at her for definition of what "better" was and found himself short. He "sought" help from a therapist and sensitive neighbor to give himself the action tools needed to improve his abrupt and abusive ways so that he could date Helen.

We are not alone in our search. That thought should be comforting on some level. If we are to egotistical, fearful, embarrassed, and "entitled" to ask for help, we will not be able to move to the next level of breaking our emotional addiction because on our own, if it was possible, we would have already done so.

In a scene from "The Lord Of The Rings Trilogy" – the second film entitled "The Two Towers" – a land called Rohan is where the following takes place. In the hall of the King, Eowyn, the niece of the King, is the only lady of the court. Her cousin ``Theodred" (the Kings son), just died from his battle wounds. She is grieving her loss when Wormtongue (a treacherous counselor to the King) comes into her chambers ad begins to weave his spell around the unprotected Eowyn.

Wormtongue: "Oh….he must have died sometime during the night. What a tragedy for the king to lose his only son and heir. I understand his passing is hard to accept. Especially now that your brother has deserted you (Wormtongue arranged for her brothers banishment).

Eowyn: "Leave me alone, Snake!"

Wormtongue: "Oh, but you are alone. Who knows what you have spoken to the darkness in bitter watches of the night when all your life seems to shrink, the walls of your bower closing in about you. A hushed, tremulsome wild thing. (He takes her face in his hands). So fair….and so cold. Like morning with pale spring, still clinging to winters chill.

Eowyn: (Pulling away from his hands) Your words are poison!"

Our emotional addiction with the negative partner thoughts and imprints we have makes sure we don't search to find who we are meant to be. Those "Wormtongue" messages bind us in the addiction and its lies to where we remain alone, isolated, and unable to escape.

CHAPTER SEVEN

"Choosing"

Choosing what we need from the search information we have gathered is critical. We haven't always made good choices, which is why we stay in our emotional addiction.

When an abuser comes into a batterer's intervention program, they begin immediately in the group to work on responsibility and consequential thinking. Making oneself responsible for harming another is paramount for change. Consequences placed by society as well as family adds to the foundation to stop those behaviors which cause the abuser to lose family, go to jail, go to prison, be on probation and court ordered for the intervention program, parenting and anger management to name just a few things.

To begin to make good choices, we must think things through all the way to the end. If I do this then what will happen; who will it affect; what impact will it have on me; will this choice enhance my life or will it cause a negative impact on my life.

A lady named Sarah was married to a man who was addicted to sex. Sarah and her husband had two daughters who had both been seeing therapists for eating disorders, depression, and other negative things. Sarah's husband traveled a lot and was home every couple weeks for 2-3 days at a time and then off traveling again.

Sarah had enrolled in my support group for victims of abuse and was finding that smoking marijuana was an addiction she had that she did not want to give up as it "took the edge off." When I asked her to explain what she meant she told me that her mind raced and the pot slowed it down. She also told the group that it helped her to cope with her relationship problems and family problems. Pot "smoothed her out" and made her less angry, she said. She didn't know at this point that her husband was a sex addict but did know things weren't good at home. She knew that her relationship was far from what she had hoped, needed or wanted it to be.

One afternoon at group, Sarah walked in with puffy, swollen eyes and a box of Kleenex. She sighed deeply, stated with anger and the emotion of having been betrayed, "You won't BELIEVE what my husband has done to me! He has porn on his computer,

porn in his briefcase and other things I don't want to mention. I'm so disgusted, angry, betrayed and I want to hurt him like he has hurt me. I can't believe that I am living with a man who has been looking at porn without my knowledge!" Still not taking a breath long enough for anyone to break into the conversation she continued on, "I also found on his computer messages from another woman to him about their relationship and how much she loved him. His replies were of how he was looking forward to moving in with her in the near future and having a life with her as well. She even had the nerve to say she was looking forward to being married to him!" At this point, she started sobbing and the weight of it all made her shoulders sag as she bent with sadness. All the women in the group immediately began supporting and comforting her. She was in need of as much of this as she could receive.

The next week Sarah's husband was diagnosed with sex addiction and entered an outpatient program, which involved her attending the family meetings at the treatment center. Her emotions of betrayal and anger was too much for her to move past and she refused to forgive the addictive behavior her husband was working on overcoming and decided that she wanted to punish him. She wanted him in as much pain as she was. Sarah chose to stay with her husband and not change her behaviors and environment, which were part of keeping the whole family in dysfunction. Her entitlement to vindictiveness, anger, and justification for her bad behaviors towards him created new emotional pathways of her own addiction to him and her marijuana.

Sarah's choices were not choices of healing, healthiness, or forgiveness for herself, her husband, and her children. Her pot use increased, her weight increased, her attendance at the women's support group slowly evaporated to where she stopped coming entirely. She stated that the group made her feel depressed and so she couldn't come anymore. Her decision for herself was in direct contradiction to the women's recovery process and so she once again blamed and justified her own addictive behaviors and choices. She was stuck in her emotional addiction to her husband, to her anger, to the relationship of a dysfunctional family where she knew who had what role, and to her pain.

Forgiveness of self and others is a choice we need to make in order to move forward and break the power and control over emotional addiction.

The 12 Step AA program states "God grant me the courage to change the things I can, to accept the things I can not change, and the wisdom to know the difference." There is a story that goes like this: "Imagine that you are walking into a completely dark room. You keep bumping into things and bruising yourself. You keep trying to do it differently...maybe walking in to the right or in to the left. You try one entrance after another and the same thing keeps happening. More bruises and bangs and scars as you bang into tables, chairs and other furniture. You can try this over and over again and achieve the same results.

Maybe you decide that if you walk in on a Tuesday, it will be different. Or on Friday afternoon. Or with a friend on a Thursday morning.

Or…..you can try a different approach. You can change your approach!

YOU CAN TURN A LIGHT ON!!!!!

You can put a light on each piece of furniture that you have been bumping and MOVE THE FURNITURE! You can live in the dark room and keep bumping into things and after enough pain, surrender to your circumstances or you could turn a light on and look at one thing in your life and begin to work on it."

All of us have areas in our life that we stumble over, into, and defects that we are not proud of. But we must choose to remove them one at a time and turn the lights on so that we can see clearly as we make room in our lives for things we don't stumble and fall over. What is blocking you from your freedom? What denials and justifications are you using to entitle yourself to continue doing the same things over and over and over? Once you can see the obstacles in your room, you will also find that you have a door in that room and the key that fits it so when you unlock it, and walk out, your new way is not one that is dark, hidden, and filled with the same obstacles to bump into. We learn from every experience and take a new ACTION so that we get different results. Remember, awareness + action = change.

> "When we discover the still, quiet place that lies within each of us, we can see it as a base to untangle ourselves from the doubt, indecision, ill health, guilt and other forms of old programming that result in confused and actions."
>
> Hallie Iglehart, Woman Spirit

CHAPTER EIGHT

Forgiveness

"In pursuit of happiness, the difficulty lies in knowing when you have caught up."   R.H. Grenville

"I won't forgive him because it means that what he did is okay and he doesn't have to be responsible" – this is the mantra that most women tell me when talking about their husbands. "I can't and I won't forget, ever, that he caused me the pain and no one can tell me otherwise."

Where did we get the idea that forgiveness means letting ourselves forget a harm or hurt that was caused by someone towards us? Religious leaders don't help when they tell victims of abuse to "turn the other cheek" or "a good Christian prays harder for a wife/husband who is harming him/her" or "God says Justice is mine, so let God take care of him and you just stay with him/her until God decides what and when to do something." We should not forget experiences that happen to us because we learn from those experiences. They teach us to not repeat the events that caused them in the first place and when the warning flags start waving, we need to seek ways to get away from the point of pain or trauma.

One of the steps necessary to break emotional addiction is this benefactory act of forgiveness. Forgiveness is integral to emotional healing and recovery from anger and hurt. An empirical study of these therapies (Friedman & Enright, 1996) begins to unfold consistently demonstrated salient positive effects on level of forgiveness and on the mental health of individuals.

Forgiveness is important and helpful for moving forward from addiction and abuse. From his clinical practice, Fitzgibbons (1996) reported that forgiveness counseling seemed to reduce anger, anxiety, and psychological depression in his clients. He found that as clients learned to forgive, they also learned to express anger in more appropriate ways.

Forgiveness has been defined another fabulous way – the willful giving up of resentment in the face of another's (or others) considerable injustice and responding with beneficence to the offender even though that offender has no right to the forgiver's moral goodness. Forgiveness is an act freely chosen by the forgiver.

Does forgiveness mean condoning, excusing or forgetting? No it doesn't. When one condones or excuses another, there is no perceived unfairness. Reconciliation involves beneficence in the face of unfairness. Forgiveness is one person's choice to let go of resentment, addictions and deeply held anger so that a person can move on. This forgiveness applies to oneself as well.

The philosopher Neblett (1974) argued that the essence of forgiveness is in the decision to forgive along with the proclamation "I forgive you." As the person decides to forgive and give the "I forgive you" proclamation, important things happen.

First, according to Baskin and Enright (2004), the forgiver has crossed an important line. He/she has moved from a position of resentment to one of letting the resentment go and not dominating their thoughts. Even though they may still have some resentment, it will not be all consuming.

Second, the forgiver is aware of their new "position" as forgiver and that there is another that is "forgiven" and that their relationship will be decided by the forgiver. This is a cognitive awareness, which also allows us to move from "victim" into "thriver."

The old saying, "To err is human, to forgive is divine," truly knew that to become a "forgiver" would have powerful effects on the process of recovery for the "forgiver."

In the movie "Sex and the City" the character that Sarah Jessica Parker plays broke up with her fiancé, "Mr. Big." Prior to the breakup, she had a photo shoot for Vogue Magazine where she wore several different wedding dresses. Then when she broke up with Mr. Big for not showing up at the wedding, her character stated that she had "emotional clutter" regarding Mr. Big. She didn't want to see the pictures anymore and stated that she was going to make changes in her life.

Our emotional clutter or addiction comes from not only memories we have but from our ancestry as well. Stop and think about it for a minute. Our bodies are created from our parent's bodies – we look like our parents and we also have similar traumas as our parents. To take this a little further, our parent's bodies came from their parents and on and on. The color of our eyes, our hair, our body structure, the shape of our heads and feet, are all legacy of both ancestors and parents. Our bodies have living histories, which we call cellular memory as already described.

The thoughts, feelings, and allergies you have may come from the results of your ancestors who had traumas that they never got over or allergens their cells couldn't handle.

CHAPTER NINE

Resilience and Abuse

*In pursuit of happiness, the difficulty lies in
knowing when you have caught up.*

-R.H. Grenville

What is resilience? Why is it important?
Resilience is the power to cope with adversity and
adapt to challenges or change. It is a process of
drawing on beliefs, behaviors, skills, and attitudes
to move beyond stress, trauma, or tragedy.
Although naturally stronger in some personalities, it
can also be learned. Resilient people have a range of
strengths such as optimism, self-knowledge,
personal meaning, and the ability to foster
relationships and care for themselves and others. By
mobilizing these powers, they confront life's
obstacles and emerge with greater wisdom,
flexibility, and strength.

So let's talk about why resilience matters. Life
doesn't always go the way we wish or expect. When
problems arise like domestic violence in our homes,

relationships end, stressors change, children change, abused women worry more, have larger fears, believe less in themselves, believe the lies they have been told by their abuser, experience anxiety and depression, have increased health concerns, and on and on. Life is out of control and the unknown is looming in front of them with all the eyes of the big green monster called fear looking back at them. They are simply in most cases overwhelmed. But what survivors don't stop to consider due to being so overwhelmed with changes is that they have resilience.

The ability to adapt to challenges and changes is known as resilience. Survivors know how to adapt to challenges and changes due to living or having lived in an abusive relationship. What they don't know is that they are using resilience. Being resilient means that they learned skills to maneuver around the tension rising phase of their relationship.

In abusive relationships there are 3 phases – Tension rising phase, Event phase, and the Honeymoon phase. Tension rising phase means that they feel like they are walking on eggshells because they know an abusive event is going to happen – they just don't know when. Being resilient means learning how to survive the event when it does happen (if they aren't killed by the event), and resilience means that during the honeymoon phase of this cycle of violence - they took care of themselves during the calm and got ready for the tension rising phase to come around again. They learn to navigate no matter what comes their way.

But when the survivor leaves a relationship, there is a disconnect from what they have been doing to survive the abusive relationship and using those resilience skills already in use to help them after leaving. In recovery, one taps into this area of a woman's (or man's) life and empowers her/him to remember the skills she/he has, learn new skills to add to the resilience used to survive and reframes them to move and motivate her/him forward to reach their educational goals, professional goals and life goals – independent of a man/woman and fully in charge of their life, their future and their children's futures.

I mentioned Optimism as being a source of resilience. Optimism is important because it gives you the capacity to focus on stressful life events and to envision a solution for those events. It means the ability to cope and plan, rather than to avoid and hide. Optimistic people accept their reactions to problems and attempt to work through them. They grieve and struggle but can still move in a positive direction, seeing problems that are severe and painful, as surmountable.

Optimism instills a sense of hope, it offers a belief that things can get better, and trust in self. Optimistic people live longer and do better works because it enables one to make choices, follow through and let go of things they can't control. For some this is natural and for some it is learned.

Healthy coping is another key element needed for building resilience. We need to have balance between negative and positive emotions and feelings. Coping is the process of deliberately taking action to create and maintain balance. It means paying attention to your physical, emotional, mental and spiritual needs so that the balance will cause health and happiness.

Self-knowledge is important to resilience because it means you know and accept yourself as you are, even if the process sometimes makes you uncomfortable. It means you identify your strengths and your weaknesses and work on the weakness to maximize your strengths. Self-knowledge helps you to learn who you are and how you feel rather than trying to become something you think others want you to be. Self-knowledge fosters resilience and self-confidence.

Personal meaning is about identifying the most important elements and values of your life. It is about exploring your worldviews, identifying your values and finding ways to put those values into practice. Personal meaning must be found – it cannot be given. It is discovered rather than invented. Personal meaning is rooted in freedom – the freedom to choose one's attitude in any given set of circumstance, to choose one's own way." People find meaning in choosing their path, which has in turn, provides profound effects on lives.

Healthy relationships with family and friends and being part of an extended "social system" at home, work, and in the community also build resilience. Soroptimist International Club for women is an example of a social system that helps build resilience. The members are women who bring strong social networks to the club; who foster relationships in the community and who are bound together for a common purpose and good, supporting those purposes and relationships. People in supportive, loving relationships are more likely to feel healthy, happy and satisfied with their lives and less likely to have depression, health problems and mental illness.

Strong social networks boost a person's chance of surviving life-threatening illness; create stronger, more resilient immune systems and provide a longer life for people than those without social support.

As women who are part of the solution to end violence and sexism that still keeps us from getting equal pay for equal jobs, our success is dependent on seeking the leadership roles and guiding women to listen, invest and believe in their female voice to change the imbalance of power and leadership. We as women need to reinforce our status while we continue to overcome the marginalization of women despite our expertise and experience. We cannot allow ourselves to be defined by those who dominate and control the imbalance of power. We must speak out and be the change that society needs and yes, requires from us as women, to create a better world for our daughters. We must use our voices and take a risk in being the women who change our community and world even when other women tell us to be quiet and stop rocking the boat, because that makes them feel uncomfortable and they would actually have to make a stand on something which could bring negative attention to them.

Resilience is the power to cope with adversity and adapt to challenges or change. By mobilizing these powers, we confront life's obstacles and emerge with greater wisdom, flexibility, and strength. So when you want to help a victim of abuse, you will want to have her tap into her ability to be resilient through the following methods:

1. Listen to her and her "truth" about her relationship without judgment
2. Listen to what she says as well as what she might not be saying
3. Be empathetic more than sympathetic

4. Don't put your values and judgments onto her – it is about her and not you
5. Ask her what she would like to have happen in her life to change the abuse and what first step she could take in making her wish a reality
6. Follow that by asking her when she could take that first step and if she is willing to take that first step.
7. Tell her there is a support system for her that won't tell her what she has to do but will be there to guide, support and help her along this change in her life
8. Congratulate her on the courage she has and how she has been surviving to date.
9. Don't ever do her work for her. You listen but she must take the action
10. Never tell her she must leave the relationship. If her life is being threatened, then of course tell her you would like for her to seek safety and shelter. However, if she chooses to not leave, then tell her that you are there for her whenever she does choose to leave. If you push her on the subject she will not trust you

and will find you to be someone she feels judgment from. But the minute you tell her she has to leave and she is not ready, or the abuser has instilled so much fear that she is paralyzed to leave, she will run from you and you will have lost all ability to be a support and safety person in her life.

11. Don't be a counselor without the proper training. Refer her to the professionals. If you refer her to a therapist, make sure the therapist is certified in domestic violence or has extensive training otherwise, the professional can do more harm than good by saying the wrong things and asking the victim to do things that put her deeper in harms way.

12. If you find she has "learned helplessness" which many have – keep telling her she is strong and resilient with experience and survival tools– after all – she has survived more than most women will ever have to survive in their lifetime.

Abuse can happen to anyone. Don't think that this happens to a certain type of woman or a certain culture. It can and does happen to one in three women. Resilience for battered women and their children leads to full recovery. For non-victims, resilience leads to fulfillment and self-honoring.

Domestic abuse is not a result of losing control; domestic abuse is one person intentionally trying to control another person. The abuser is purposefully using verbal, nonverbal, or physical means to gain control over the other person.

In some cultures, control of women by men is accepted as the norm. This article speaks from the orientation that control of intimate partners is domestic abuse within a culture where such control is not the norm. Today we see many cultures moving from the subordination of women to increased equality of women within relationships.

What are the types of domestic abuse?

The types of domestic abuse are:

- physical abuse (domestic violence)
- verbal or nonverbal abuse (psychological abuse, mental abuse, emotional abuse)
- sexual abuse
- stalking or cyber stalking

- economic abuse or financial abuse
- spiritual abuse

The divisions between these types of domestic abuse are somewhat fluid, but there is a strong differentiation between the various forms of physical abuse and the various types of verbal or nonverbal abuse.

What is physical abuse of a spouse or intimate partner?

Physical abuse is the use of physical force against another person in a way that ends up injuring the person, or puts the person at risk of being injured. Physical abuse ranges from physical restraint to murder. When someone talks of domestic violence, they are often referring to physical abuse of a spouse or intimate partner.

Physical assault or physical battering is a crime, whether it occurs inside a family or outside the family. The police are empowered to protect you from physical attack.

Physical abuse includes:

- pushing, throwing, kicking

- slapping, grabbing, hitting, punching, beating, tripping, battering, bruising, choking, shaking
- pinching, biting
- holding, restraining, confinement
- breaking bones
- assault with a weapon such as a knife or gun
- burning
- murder
- ice and snow (frostbite or other injuries from being kept in cold environments)

What is emotional abuse or verbal abuse of a spouse or intimate partner?

Mental, psychological, or emotional abuse can be verbal or nonverbal. Verbal or nonverbal abuse of a spouse or intimate partner consists of more subtle actions or behaviors than physical abuse. While physical abuse might seem worse, the scars of verbal and emotional abuse are deep. Studies show that verbal or nonverbal abuse can be much more emotionally damaging than physical abuse.

Psychological abuse can be hard to recognize because it doesn't produce physical scars. Yet many women agree that it is actually much harder to bear than physical abuse. Psychological abuse goes to the very core of a woman's soul and spirit. It is used by a batterer to go deep inside – to the core of womanhood and slowly, like a virus, work away at her personhood until she doubts herself to the very center of who she is. Once this is allowed to happen, it takes a journey of time and processing to rediscover herself, her likes and dislikes, and her belief systems.

Time and support from trained counselors and therapists specifically trained in domestic violence will help the survivor regain her psychological strength and create new attitudes and beliefs about relationships, parenting and self worth, putting things in healthy perspectives.

Knowing how we have emotional addiction to our abusers and how resilience can help us to overcome our unhealthy ties to the abuser is important to breaking their bonds of power and control.

CHAPTER TEN

Prologue

Addictive relationships can be hard to define, and so difficult for you to tell if you are in one. However, a bad relationship is something to take seriously and if a family member, friend, or other person connected to you tells you to consider that you might be in one – then don't discount what they are saying. If you can figure out that you are in one and your "gut" tells you something is wrong, then you are one step closer to getting out of it so that you can learn from it and move forward into a good relationship.

An addictive relationship is one that isolates one from others and the world. It is identical to drug or alcohol addiction which keeps the addict from things they love and activities they should accomplish. Emotional addiction creates a very dysfunctional relationship because it is defined by an increasing craving to be with a person and when one is not with that person, withdrawal symptoms are experienced. It has some of the same signs as other addictions such as low self-worth, passivity, helplessness, magical thinking or "eternal hope" thinking, lack of initiative and selfishness.

Here are some warning signs of being in an addictive relationship and if you recognize these or any number of them – don't walk – run away from the relationship and get help:

a. Animal Attraction: that love "at first sight" or overt infatuation. This is a red flag that should be waving high and the flapping in the wind should be deafening.

b. Desire to change the other person: if changing the other person is what you want to do then you are already losing. People won't change because you think you have the power to change them – they change because they have the power to do it and WANT to change. If you find yourself thinking that the relationship would be perfect if the person would just change a little, it is a sign of a bad relationship.

c. Unable to end a relationship: if you know that you need to leave a relationship but feel undeserving, that others will be talking about you, or your fear of being alone keeps you in it, this is a bad sign that you might be in an addictive relationship.

d. If you notice that other relationships of happy people seem boring to you, then you might be addicted to drama. Chaos in relationships sometimes keeps trauma bonding and its cycle's part of the addictive process. Check your drama and chaos experiences in your relationship – you might be addicted to them.

e. Independence: if you find that you can't be independent in the relationship but might be in other areas of your life, it might be a sign of an emotionally addictive relationship.

f. Putting partner's needs above yours: if you can't say no to your partner and you have to put their needs above yours or that they demand you put their needs above yours, you might be in an addictive relationship.

g. Feel self-doubt or unimportant: if your relationship and partner make you feel self-doubt or you are told you have no value in the relationship, then your relationship is dysfunctional and you need to get help to get out.

Addictive love patterns can be evident in all types of relationships. But most are involved in love relationships with romantic interaction. Emotional addiction can cut a person off from life. In order to have a mature love, one must identify some of the following statements to see if they believe them:

1. To be truly happy, I have to be in a relationship: otherwise I will be depressed and not accepted in society.

2. I often feel a magnetic pull towards another person even when they might not be good for me.

3. I have to change my partner to meet my ideal expectation.

4. I have a hard time letting relationships go.

5. I think my partner can't survive or function without me.

6. I need a relationship at all times, so I jump from one to another with no time between to work on myself or to

give me time to evaluation what went wrong with the first relationship.

7. I often get involved with someone who is emotionally distant, or is married or is involved with someone else.

8. I don't like kind and boring partners and usually reject them because they don't keep the relationship exciting.

9. I am fearful of being on my own and need a relationship.

10. I can't say no to the person I am involved with.

11. I don't feel worthy of a good relationship but want one but don't know how to get one.

12. I am jealous and possessive and need to maintain control.

13. I want to please my partner sexually more than myself.

14. I can't stop seeing my partner even though I know he/she is destructive to me, to my children and to our family.

15. You continue to have your thoughts controlled by memories of a relationship for months and even years after it has ended. Your "fantasy" memories are not actually the reality of how the relationship was. You focus on the "good" times and play down the "bad" behaviors and actions.

The most essential priority in breaking free from emotional addiction is to make recovery the first priority. It needs to be more important then meeting a new person, having a date, fantasizing about an ex-lover, gaining approval from family and friends, and letting go of obsessive attention to another. Breaking free of negative, self-defeating patterns learned from childhood. Define your personal boundaries so that your life is balanced, you maintain a healthy sense of self and reclaim your spiritual life, psychological life, physical life. You have the power to make choices concerning your own life and making the right choices in all areas of your life. Find a professional who can help you each step of your journey in recovery.

Fall in love with yourself and you will always have love!

References:

1. The God Gene: How Faith is Hardwired in our Gene's, Dean H. Hamer, Random House, 2005
2. Father Hunger, Margo Maine, Gurze Books, 2003
3. The Batterer as Parent, Bancroft and Silverman, Sage Publishing, 2002
4. What the Bleep Do I Know, DVD, Quantum Edition, Captured Light Distribution, 2004
5. The Genetic Gods, Avise, Captured Light Distribution DVD What the Bleep Do I know, 2004
6. Twelve Steps and Twelve Traditions, Alcoholics Anonymous World Services, 1952
7. The Journey Within, Ruth Fishel, Health Communications Inc., 1952
8. Woman Spirit, Hallie Iglehart, Harper and Row Publishers, 1983
9. Prospering Woman, Ruth Ross, Whatever Publishing Inc., 1982
10. Choice Making, Sharon Wegscheider-Cruse, Health Communications, 1985
11. Transitions, William Bridges, Addison, Wesley Publishing Company, 1980
12. Why Does He Do That?, Lundy Bancroft, L.P, Putnam's Sons, 2002
13. Captivating, John and Stasi Elderedge, Thomas-Nelson Publishing, 1993
14. The Batterer, Donald Dutton, 1993
15. It Could Happen to Anyone, Barnett and LaViolette, Sage Publications, 1993
16. The Dance of Anger, Harriet Lerner, Harper and Row, 1985
17. Victims No More, Thomas McCabe, Hazelden, 1978
18. The Addictive Personality, Craig Nakken, Harper/Collins/Hazelden, 1988

19. You are Not Alone, Grossack, Marlborough House, 1965
20. A Look at Relapse, Crewe, Hazelden, 1973
21. Aftercare: Blueprint for a Richer Life, Kimball, Hazelden, 1976
22. Help Yourself, Lembo, Argus Communications, 1974
23. Factors affecting women's decisions to leave violent relationships, Journal of Family Issues, 2, 391-414
24. Woman-battering: Victims and their experiences, Pagelow, Sage Publishing, 1981
25. Patterns of emotional bonding in battered women: Traumatic bonding. International Journal of Women's Studies, Dutton & Painter, 1985
26. Stockholm Syndrome in emotionally abused adult women, Ott, Graham & Rawlings, paper presented at annual meeting of the American Psychological Association, Boston, 1990
27. Wife's marital dependency and wife abuse, Kalmuss, Straus, Journal of Marriage and Family, 1982
28. Attachment styles of women with histories of abusive relationships, Justice and Hirt, paper presented at the annual meeting of the American Psychological Association, Washington D.C., 1992
29. Battered Women as Survivors: An alternative to treating learned helplessness, Gondolf, 1988
30. Bound by love: The sweet trap of daughterhood, Gilbert and Webster, Beacon Publishers, 1982
31. Conditioned emotional reactions, Watson and Raynor, Journal of Experimental Psychology, 3, 1-14, 1920
32. The Battered Woman Syndrome, Walker, Springer, New York, 1984
33. The Long Goodbye: Vaughn, Psychology Today, pp. 37-38, 42, July 1987

34. The "God Part of the Brain: A Scientific Interpretation of Human Spirituality and God," Alper Publishing, 2008

Recovery Work for Emotional Addiction –

Bonding for Bad Relationships

By

Kathie Mathis, Psy.D

BEGINNING RECOVERY NOW!

"Our genes can predispose us to believe. But they don't tell us what to believe in."

Choice is key. What is emotion? There are many different scientific thoughts about what an emotion is or isn't. Emotion is one of the most controversial topics in psychology, a source of intense discussion and disagreement from the earliest philosophers to thinkers of today. Most agree that emotion has "components" made up of physiological and psychological factors and include emotion faces, emotion elicitors, and emotion neural processes. A broad consensus has emerged on what we might call adequacy conditions on any theory of emotion. An acceptable philosophical theory of emotions should be able to account at least for the following nine characteristics. All the recent and current accounts of emotion discussed here have something to say about most of them, and some have had something to say about all.

- emotions are typically conscious phenomena;

- yet they typically involve more pervasive bodily manifestations than other conscious states;
- they vary along a number of dimensions: intensity, valence, type and range of intentional objects, etc.
- they are reputed to be antagonists of rationality;
- also they play an indispensable role in determining the quality of life;
- they contribute crucially to defining our ends and priorities;
- they play a crucial role in the regulation of social life;
- they protect us from an excessively slavish devotion to narrow conceptions of rationality;
- they have a central place in moral education and the moral life.

The exploration of questions raised by these nine characteristics is a thriving ongoing collaborative project in the theory of emotions, in which philosophy will continue both to inform and to draw on a wide range of philosophical expertise as well as the parallel explorations of other branches of cognitive science. (Emotions by unknown author).

At the core of common sense approaches to emotion is the one that people have in mind when talking about human emotions – the feeling component or the passion or sensation of emotion. Another obvious component is the set of behaviors that may be performed and observed in conjunction with an emotion.

Whatever your philosophy on what makes an emotion – the hope is that you find your way to believe that you can be a fulfilled person and that emotional addiction can be broken through different modalities including, choice, counseling, life experience, faith, meditation, and scientific methods. Our Emotional Addiction training book is one small way that can help you. Change is work but something so worth the effort – and it begins with a "spark."

We have been wounded into believing things about ourselves from the time we were small. We were shown by parents who had poor parenting skills that we were not smart enough, good enough, important enough, lovable enough; just not "enough" of anything to be valued by them. Our very sense of who we are is attacked before we even have formed a sense of who we are or had the opportunity to form a sense of who we are. We learned and experienced heartbreak at an early age. So why wouldn't we be screwed up as an adult. Our lives needed to begin with the knowledge that our fathers cherished us and that our mothers loved us and both of them wanted us and at least, wanted to spend some time with us. Their jobs of making us feel good, enjoyed, treasured and safe as well as "enough" seems an overwhelming chore to adults who have abuse, addictions, and other issues that keep them from this very important duty and responsibility. So our hearts and souls have empty spaces that were formed and we ache to be treasured, honored, cherished, and loved and most of all "enough."

Deep within every human being lies the true spirit essence of our being, an energy or spark that gives us all our sameness and connection. Recent research has shown that in all blue-eyed individuals there is something in the eye gene that is "exactly" the same in all blue-eyed individuals showing that all blue-eyed humans are related. The scientists will probably find the same in all brown-eyed humans. What make us different are our experiences - experiences that we have throughout our life times and those that are genetically passed on to us by our ancestors. Each moment we experience of life after birth will ignite the spark within us or cover it. The good news is that no matter what we experience with drugs, abuse, food, relationships and "life events," we will always have a bit of that "spark" waiting to re-ignite. Love, compassion, honoring, kindness, caring and nurturing will make it glow, lighting up the coldest and loneliest places in our heart and spirit.

Here is the reason you we want you to know what emotional addiction is so you can know that the healing of your heart is available and that our desire is to help you on your journey to find that healing. To help you overcome hurts and pains and to release emotional addiction created by those experiences, restoring your life to a healthier level so you can flourish and become happier is the goal of a emotional addiction counselor, coach and advocate.

EMOTIONAL HEALTH

So how does one improve their emotional health? First, take time to recognize and understand why you are having certain emotions. Being able to sort them out helps identify causes of sadness, stress and anxiety in your life and helps you to manage your emotional health.

Express your feelings appropriately and don't stuff them down inside. It's okay to let your family know when something is bothering you but keep in mind that they may not be able to help you deal with those feelings. So at this time ask someone trained to help you such as a counselor, doctor, religious advisor, or therapist for advice and support. This will improve your coping abilities as well as your emotional health.

Try not to:
1. Obsess about problems and live a balanced life
2. Deal with negative feelings, but try to focus on the positive things in life as well

Try to:

3. Find ways to deal with balance of mind, body and soul
4. Have good health - it is important to emotional health and good decision-making

Ways to balance mind, body and soul!

It is easy to say find way to balance mind, body and soul. But lets explore some of the ways that we can accomplish this.

Ways to have and keep good health!

RELATIONAL WOMEN

Most all women are relationally based. From the time we are small, we develop relationships with other girls, our dolls, our pets and especially our mothers and fathers. Our sense of self and how we see ourselves as grown women is shaped by our early relationships as little girls. Our mothers teach us what it means to be a woman and our fathers teach us the value we have as a woman. Our relationship with others teach us what the world thinks of us.

Society says women should be:

Society says women should not be:

For centuries women have lived with relational fellowship with other women. We gathered and gossiped at the river as we did laundry. We talked to each other over fences while we hung our laundry on the clothesline to dry. We met at wells as we filled our water jugs and discussed the politics of the day. When young women were in accompaniment of their mothers or older sisters, information on what it meant to be a woman and what femininity is, was passed along naturally. It was a means of "passage" where women gathered information on the men in the community, business in the community, religion in the community and the culture in which they were to live. These times were stamped into women's relationship memory book – their brain.

In today's world most of us don't go to the well to draw water, or to the river to wash our clothes (however in some countries these practices still take place). Most of us have clothes dryers, washing machines, running water in our houses, and other modern conveniences. When we meet women it is in church, at the PTA, at committee meetings, or at Mommy and Me classes. Agenda's, rigid time constrictions set activities, deadlines, and other modern problems like grid lock, two jobs, and more, keep us from experiencing the "relational" learning, socializing, and passage turning from little girls into women. So we watch and learn from our mothers, grandmothers and other adult women in our lives if they have the time to be relational with us but mostly we learn from television and the movies.

Make a list of some of the things you were taught from your families as to how you were to live your life:

Mothers and fathers need to be present, need to enjoy, and to love and hug lavishly. They need to be tender with their children's souls and emotions, to have close and caring relationships with them.

What do you think Unconditional Positive Regard is? How does it relate to our relationship with family members?

Studies have shown that women who have reported having close and caring relationships with their fathers and mothers suffer less eating disorders, depression, addictions, illness and anxieties. They had a "strong sense of personal identity and positive self esteem." (Margo Maine, Father Hunger).

What was your relationship like with your mother?

What actions and/or words did she use to let you know she was "present" in your life and that she was holding your tender spirit with unconditional positive regard?

What was your relationship like with your father?

What actions and/or words did he use to let you know he was "present" in your life and that he was holding your tender spirit with unconditional positive regard?

"There can be no knowledge without emotion. We may be aware of a truth, yet until we have felt its force, it is not ours. To

the cognition of the brain must be added
the experience of the soul."
Arnold Bennett (1867-1931)

Trauma Bonding/Love Confusion

Those of us who didn't have loving, caring, and emotionally and physically present parents as we were growing up were born just like everyone else, with this "spark" in our souls but with early experiences that left us hurting. Our parents brought into our early lives deprivation of "connection" to them in the form of inconsistent love (trauma bonding), deprivation of love, and everything in between. Their gift to us was their guilt's, fears, hang-ups, abuse, addictions and genetic problems. And we took it all in, absorbed it like a sponge, and made decisions about ourselves like we were not valued because we were told to "shut up," "leave me alone," "you're an idiot like your mother," or "like your father" and so on. We made oaths that we would not be like our mothers or fathers as we dreamed of escaping and finding someone or something to love us and give us back the "spark" that was slowly being smothered in our lives. So we begin seeking those things in fill our lives that will fill us up and make the "spark" return. And the choices we make are not always the ones with positive outcomes.

Name choices you have made to try and fill up the "hole" in your soul and create a "spark" that will bring you fulfillment but were negative choices:

What did you learn from those choices?

Important steps to emotional well-being:

1. The level of bonding between a parent and child is extremely important to the
Well-being and self-esteem of a child and emotional addiction.

2. Factors that can help re-ignite the inner spark of a young person are the development of talents, interests, and relationships with trustworthy adults.

3. When adults empower a child with words like, "your special," or "you are so smart" or "you make

me so proud" then children's inner spark is ignited into limitless possibilities. 4. Choices in letting go of self-blame, negative influences and messages. 5.Creating strengths in peer relationships with positive influences.

6. Create nurturing and resilience while developing personal strengths and reducing trauma bonding.

7. Resilience is the power to cope with adversity and adapt to challenges or change. It is a process of drawing on beliefs, behaviors, skills, and attitudes to move beyond stress, trauma, or tragedy. Although naturally stronger in some personalities, it can also be learned.

8. Focus energies on creating love instead of criticism and anger. strengths such as optimism, self-knowledge, personal meaning , and the ability to foster relationships and care for themselves and others. By mobilizing these powers, they will confront life's obstacles and emerge with greater wisdom, flexibility, and strength.

Negative steps to emotional harm:
1.Systematic abuse – particularly of a kind that involves cycles of intermittent fear and kindness –

can lead to the formation of unusually strong but unhealthy bonds and can foster the victim's development of potent dependence on the abuser (Dutton, 1995; James, 1994; Dutton & Painter, 1993; Herman, 1992).

2. Effects of abuse create a potent longing in the victim for kindness and understanding, and for relief from the fear or terror experienced (Dutton & Painter, 1993). A person who is able to provide soothing treatment at the right moment will tend to be perceived by the victim as a rescuer, and so to be looked upon with gratitude.

3. In traumatic bonding, the person who brings the soothing relief is the same one who perpetrated the abuse.

4. Following an incident of abuse, for example, an abuser may apologize for what happened, express concern for how the victim is feeling, and speak in a calm and warm tone. The typical response in victims of abuse is to feel thankful for the kindness, to be eager to forgive, and to form a belief that the abuser actually cares deeply for him or her. Once this cycle has been repeated a number of times, the victim may come to feel

grateful to the abuser for just stopping the abuse each time, even if no real kindness or attentiveness follows. This has been demonstrated to be a normal response to abuse related trauma in males and in females (Herman, 1992) rather than a masochistic trait in females as was assumed previously, and the intermittency of the abuse has been demonstrated to be a critical reason for the strength of trauma bonds (Dutton & Painter, 1993) (Bancroft & Silverman, 2002)."

5. Children and adults can become bonded to and protectors of their abusers. They can gradually become love confused just like the abuser. Because the "loving behavior" follows so closely the "trauma" behavior, the two become psychologically and emotionally linked in the victim's brain (Dutton & Painter, 1993).

6.Traumatic bonding leads the child to become increasingly focused "on the needs, wants, and emotional state of the abusive adult (which)....causes the child to lose focus on developing his or her abilities or engaging with the world (Whitten, 1994, p.35).

7. List some other negatives in harming one's emotional well being:

"Someday, after we have mastered the winds, the waves,
the tides and gravity, we shall harness for God the energies of love. Then, for the second time in the history of the world, man will have discovered fire."

Teilhard de Chardin

The Brain – What we don't see!

Studies have shown that 75% of the information our brains take in a day is negative information and 25% is positive information. The horrors that abusive mothers and fathers have on young lives and the wounds imprinted in our brains goes to the very core of our souls. It breaks hearts, heaps shame, and creates feelings of unworthiness, un-love-ableness, minimization of self, valueless. Along with other negative experiences and messages, it makes us emotionally ill as well as physically ill. It strips us of our natural spirit self and leaves us sick, broken, empty, and damaged to the point that we don't know who we are and what we want.

But some of what we experience doesn't manifest itself in this manner and remains unseen and is equally, if not more, damaging. If we don't understand or know about emotional shame then how can we trust it? If we haven't acknowledged our fears, how can we overcome them? If our lives are unmanageable and out of control, and we don't stop to take care of it and keep stuffing more into it hoping no one notices – how can we expect our relationships with our partners, children, friends, family, bosses – and most importantly ourselves, to be fulfilling?

What is emotional shame?
What fears have we not acknowledged?
Where in our life do we feel we have things that are unmanageable?

Our hearts desire is to be loved and amazing to our partner. We want to be "enough" and not "too much" or "too controlling" or too critical, over bearing, aggressive, sexual, overweight, loud, thin and so on....! We want to be "enough" yet outside messages tell us we are to be more – to be "perfect" and so we wear our masks and hide our true spirit and self. Our emotional addiction comes to be our friend to give us feelings of "perfectness" or "wholeness" or "enough".

List some messages we receive about being "perfect":

What messages have we given ourselves if we don't fit the messages we have received about being perfect?

HOW WE BECOME ADDICTED TO AN EMOTION!

Our body uses combinations of special chemicals to produce each of the different emotions. Do you know that there is a certain chemical combination for happiness, and sadness, and anger, and victimization, and any other emotion that you can think of?

Throughout the years, people develop an addiction to the different chemicals of different emotions. **The point is the more people feel a certain emotion, the more addicted to that emotion they become.** For example, if you get angry on a consistent basis, you develop an emotional addiction to the anger chemicals. And if you play a victim and cry why you long enough, you habituate that way of being and develop an emotional addiction to those specific chemicals. As each of the cells divides, the new cells created need more and more of those specific chemicals in order to get the same stimulation as the old cell.

So how does this all connect with the law of attraction? Our usual emotional state attracts to us more of that emotional state. So you can see that if we are addicted to specific emotional states, we have to undo the habitual addiction to those negative emotional states and develop new behaviors and habits for the positive emotional chemicals. Thus, people often will act in particular ways just to get the fix of their emotional addiction. The real difficulty for many people is to get past emotional addictions and develop more productive and positive emotional addictions. You have to will to practice new behaviors in order to develop new habits and therefore new emotional and positive emotions.

WAYS IN WHICH WE CAN CHANGE NEGATIVE EMOTIONAL THOUGHTS TO NEW POSITIVE EMOTIONAL THOUGHTS

1. Affirmations
2. Journaling
3. Guided Imagery
4. Relaxation and Breathing Exercises
5. Alpha State
6. Your choice

AFFIRMATIONS:

Studies show that it takes from 27 days up to 3 months to change an attitude/behavior doing 50 affirmations or more a day.

This process is very difficult the first time; nevertheless, with enough practice it becomes permanent and then easy to stay happy because of your addiction to that particular positive emotional condition. The point is - the more you practice those positive emotions - the easier it gets over time because your body will naturally develop an addiction for those emotional chemicals and attract situations and people to you in order to maintain that emotional addiction. Practice positive emotions, and eventually the universe will throw situations and people at you in order to maintain that emotional addiction.

You can't look to others for validation of your inner spirit and soul. No one can tell you who you are as a woman, a man, a person. And no one can give you a verdict on who you are even though they may want to be your judge and jury. They are not reliable, honest, and safe sources. But you can validate who you are. You can break emotional addiction and honor your personhood. So let's look at how to begin this more fully.

BREAKING EMOTIONAL ADDICTION

Dean Hamer, author of "The God Gene" began looking in 1998, when he was conducting a survey on smoking and addiction for the National Cancer Institute. As part of his study, he recruited over 1,000 women and men who agreed to take a standardized, 240 question personality test called the Temperament and Character Inventory (TCI). Among the traits the TCI measures is one known as self-transcendence, which consists of three other traits: self-forgetfulness (the ability to get entirely lost in an experience); transpersonal identification (feeling connectedness to a larger universe); and mysticism (openness to things not literally provable). Put these all together and science comes as close as it can to measuring what it feels like to be spiritual.

"This allows us to have the kind of experience described as religious ecstasy," says Robert Cloninger, Washington University psychiatrist and designer of the transcendence portion of the TCI.

Hamer decided to use the data he gathered in the smoking survey to conduct a little spirituality study on the side. He first ranked the participants among Cloninger's self-transcendence scale placing them on a continuum from least to most spiritually inclined. Then he studied their genes to see if he could find the DNA responsible for the differences. No easy task with 35,000 genes consisting of 3.2 billion chemical bases. So to narrow the field, Hamer confined his work to nine specific genes known to play major roles in production of monoamines – brain chemicals, including serotonin, nor epinephrine and dopamine that regulate such fundamental functions as mood and motor control. It's monoamines that are carefully manipulated by Prozac and other antidepressants.

Studying the nine candidate genes in DNA samples provided by the study subjects, Hamer hit the genetic markers. A variation in a gene known as vmal2 – for vesicular monoamine transporter – seemed to be directly related to how the volunteers scored on the self-transcendence test. Those with the nucleic acid cytosine in one particular spot on the gene ranked higher than those with the nucleic acid adenine in the same spot. "A single change in the single base in the middle of the gene seemed directly related to the ability to feel self-transcendence," Hamer stated. Merely having that feeling did not mean

those people would take the next step and translate their transcendence into a belief in – or even a quest for – God, but they seemed likelier to do so.

Hamer was careful to point out that the gene he found is by no means the only one that affects spirituality. Even minor human traits can be governed by the interplay of many genes. A complex belief possibly could involve hundreds, if not more, genes.

Hamer stressed that while he may have located a genetic root for spirituality that it is not the same as a genetic root for religion. Spirituality is a feeling or state of mind; religion is the way that states get manifested.

1. Understanding a bit of the emotional connection many have to their religion is now better understood. Hamer puts it this way, "Spirituality is intensely personal; religion is institutional."

2. Neuroscientist Andrew Newberg of the University of Pennsylvania School of

Medicine researched how spirituality plays out in the brain. He used several types of imaging systems to watch brains of subjects as they meditate or pray. By measuring blood flow, he determines which regions are responsible for the feelings the volunteers experienced. The deeper the subjects descended into meditation or prayer, the more active the frontal lobe and the limbic system became. The frontal lobe is the seat of concentration and attention and the limbic system is where our powerful feelings, including rapture, are processed. More revealing is the fact that at the same time these regions flash to life, another important region in the back of the brain – the parietal lobe – goes dim. It's this lobe that orients the individual in time and space. Take it off-line and the boundaries of the self fall away creating a feeling of being one with the universe. When you combine that with what is going on in the other two lobes, you can have a profound spiritual experience.

3. Avise wrote in the book "The Genetic Gods" that genes have special powers over human lives and affairs. The genetic material in organisms alive today traces back generation to generation through an unbroken chain of descent (with modifications) from ancestral molecules that have copied and replaced themselves ever since the origin of life on earth, about 4 billion years ago."

4. Hamer stated that more research has to be done to determine more gene responsibilities in humans." Women seem to score higher than men on transcendence tests and he believed this was true because women are more attuned to their emotional connections.

5.Emotional addiction then comes from genetics, ancestry, behaviors and attitudes, and connections or lack of to our spirituality. Emotional addiction is the condition of being habitually or compulsively occupied with or involved in something.

Recovery from any addiction is work. Finding a professional to discuss your emotional addictions in conjunction with other recovery tools like meditation, yoga, 12 step programs, exercise, focusing inward instead of outward on the person you are addicted to, and journaling, is suggested.

JOURNALING (Taken from HealthWomensHealthyLivingandgoals.com):

Learning how to journal is perhaps one of the biggest self- empowering steps you can take.

As well as helping you to realize your life goals and ambitions, personal journaling has been proven to be an effective self help tool which can also improve your emotional and physical health.

This journal guide is designed to help you gain insights into how to journal for your ideas and solutions, using your conscious and subconscious mind.

I have often stressed throughout this site, the importance of using your journal to record your goal setting activities, as well as your thoughts, feelings and awareness of the goal setting process. The following will provide you with further in-depth guidance on journaling your goal setting for maximum success.

You'll find the following an excellent resource on focused, purposeful Journaling and journal writing tools for self empowerment.

Journaling Overview

The word journal or journaling will hold different meanings for different people. Journal writing is one of the most beneficial and powerful things you can do in your day to day life. The journaling process has several distinct benefits. These are:-

· Journaling provides an outlet for feelings and emotions, e.g. fear, anxiety, confusion, doubt, anger, inadequacy, guilt, worry etc.,

· Journal writing becomes a tool for logging your day to day experiences, personal goals, and goal setting activities, your progress and achievements for your own self-analysis

· Journaling helps you to tap into and bring into awareness, a rich source of information and ideas from both your conscious and subconscious

· When you journal write, your notes provide valid feedback on your hopes, expectations, goal setting results, as well as heightening your insights and awareness on how to expand on your achievements

· Learning how to journal is one of the biggest steps you can take toward self empowerment, since what you'll discover can only reinforce that your ideas, solutions have come from you alone - helping you to build on your level of self-trust, self- belief and self-reliance.

Journaling with structure

All you'll need to record your journal entries is a notebook or a binder with loose leaf format and a pen. You can also use a diary, although the limited number of pages will prohibit the amount you write. If you prefer, you can purchase a book specifically for this purpose, although any writing material will suffice.

There is no need to worry about your grammar, spelling or use of punctuations since the issue of importance is to bring to your attention, your personal experiences and feeling.

Knowing how to journal with structure will make the process that much easier and enable you to locate your dated journal entries much later on. Just as a book will have a table of contents for easy navigation, you might also want to set aside a number of pages at the beginning of your journal, to help you locate your entries with ease later on.

Do find yourself a quiet corner where you won't be disturbed or interrupted. Pay attention to - and observe all the things that help you to feel relaxed and centered. Have a glass of water or a few nibbles to hand for example.

Journaling the processes you're working through:

Journaling isn't a difficult process; nor is being a good writer or having good writing skills a prerequisite of journal writing. What's important is that you develop a style that suits you and which you're comfortable with. You'll find that as you progress with your writing, your journaling skills will also develop.

Journal writing is a process of expressing your feelings and experiences, thus creating movement within you. This movement will stimulate your creativity thinking and open windows of ideas, notions, and insights as to how to surmount challenges to your goals.

You can enhance your journal learning by following these basic guidelines:

- do record journal entries by dating each one
- Your journal writing entries should also include the time, place, the emotions you're

experiencing, your moods etc., This is an important inclusion which will later throw light on the processes when you review your journal entry

· The best way to record journal entries is to write at speed, noting the first thoughts ideas, feelings or emotions that pops into your head. This data is 'raw' and is more likely to contain the key to solutions/how and what you're experiencing, as opposed to when you're being more thoughtful or actively thinking.

· if you find yourself hesitant or of wanting to erase or amend your journal writing, this could be indicative of your comfort zone being under threat from writing about something you might sub-consciously want to avoid. Just leave it alone and restart a fresh paragraph. You can later return to analyze this further to ascertain the issue you're avoiding and how to best deal with it.

Journaling techniques:

There are numerous techniques on how to journal write. Here are a few you might want to consider. You might even find that you have your own personal style already. Either way, the following journaling techniques offer a guide as to what you can do.

How to journal write the 'Reflective' way:

Using this style of journal writing, aim to record from an **'observer'** perspective, by replacing 'I' with 'she'. For example, instead of starting an entry with, 'I decided this wasn't a good move for me to make', write it as if you are commenting on an observation you have made - e.g. 'it would appear that her decision did not best warrant that situation. Continue your personal journaling with a detailed account of events, including 'her' recollection of scents, sounds, sights, emotions, feelings, etc., By taking the 'I' (yourself) out of the loop, you become more objective and effective in your journal writing.

Journal writing the 'clustering' way:

Personal journaling using the 'clustering' approach is very effective when you experience writing blocks or you find that your thoughts don't flow for you to record them. Start by writing the subject of your recording in the middle of the page. Circle it to make it stand out and immediately proceed in making associations with the subject. As each idea emerge, draw a circle around it and link it with a line to the main subject. This is a simple yet effective method that will present you with an array of ideas that will surprise you. You can later develop each circle into a new expanded version or simply leave them as they are.

Another good 'how to journal' technique for when you encounter 'writer's block', is to record how you're presently feeling, or simply describe an event or even a conversation you've had. Once you start, you'll find your writing begins to flow.

Journaling the 'unsent letter' way:

This is a very empowering 'how to journal' technique that will help you to freely express what/how you're experiencing. Whether your experience is related to an event, a situation, an individual or even to yourself, this 'how to journal' letter style provides a platform for you to speak out, especially if you're less than comfortable with a more direct, face to face approach. Your 'unsent letter' if for your own purposes and is therefore not actually sent.

Simply start your letter in exactly the same way as you would any other letter, addressing the person or situation by name. You'll be amazed by the amount and quality of what you communicate on paper.

You might find this technique useful when learning how to journal write your assertiveness and your communication skills. For example you might have a goal to build your assertiveness with your partner or an employer. By writing to him/her about how his/her actions or behaviors undermine and impact on your level of assertiveness, can also help bring to your attention your own responses and how you can go about changing and/or developing them more appropriately for you.

Journal writing the 'Cathartic' way:

Having the security of a safe and trusting environment in which you can truly express all your deepest fears and concerns isn't always easy to come by. Your personal journaling however, will always provide you with this much needed space. Learning how to journal strong emotions such as anger, frustration, pain, fear or worry is a very liberating experience. Furthermore, your personal journal won't raise an eyebrow, or feed back disapproval, criticize you or even cast judgment on you. Your journal or diary frees you to hammer away and get it all out in the open. A suggestion to start off this area of your journal is to open with a sentence such as - 'I am presently feeling....'. Allow your writing to flow thereon, without limiting yourself in your writing. At the journal review stage, you might well find that having put it all down on paper, you now don't want to hold on to these particular recordings. Discretely disposing of the page can be symbolic of getting rid of the negative emotions once and for all.

How to journal your goal setting activities:

Personal Goal Setting has already been addressed elsewhere so this section is specifically related to how to journal your goal setting activities.

Learning how to journal your goals involve developing a relationship with your journal; one that is tailored to your needs and aims. Treat your journal or diary as your personal coach.

You determine your goals and actions and your journal (coach) will help you formulate ideas and insights in such a way that they have every possible chance of being achieved.

Get creative with the journaling techniques you use, why you're using them and your journal will be supportive of your efforts.

How to journal attentively:

A most important feature of how to journal your goal setting activities, is learning to take yourself, your aims, your experiences and your unconscious resourcefulness seriously. This means, setting aside time to communicate with your journal on a regular basis.

Being attentive means approaching your goals activity journaling with thoughtfulness. That is, noting the ideas, notions and strategies that emerge out of your journaling and acting upon them. This will help you to explore yourself and to find out what makes you tick, your areas of strength as well as how to build your development areas.

With the right approach you'll develop your skills in how to journal your goals and get the most out of your efforts. For example, rather than feel overwhelmed by one of your more ambitious targets, journaling can help you breakdown larger long term goals into smaller short-term achievable steps.

It stops you from feeling overwhelmed by the enormity of your goal. For example, start by writing about where you'd ideally want to be in any aspect of your life in 5 years time. You'll be amazed by the quality and quantity of ideas and insights you gain as to the medium-term and short-term steps you'll need to take as well as how to journal the actions you'll need to get you there.

How to journal using images:

The different ways in how to journal is only limited by your imagination. Once you've set your goals, use your journal to scrapbook images, snippets of pictures you've cut out from magazines, or even drawings etc., to reinforce and strengthen your motivation toward achieving your goals.

Lets say for instance that you have a weight loss goal. You've already journaled your feelings and thoughts on what it will mean to you to attain a certain weight or to look a certain way; by cutting out images from magazines or using old photos of yourself and how you ideally want to look, every time you open your journal you'll be greeted by these images which are a positive statement of intent of where you want to be.

Here's another example, using that same weight loss goal; in support of you, your partner has promised you a world cruise once you've attained your goal. Again, if every time you open your journal, you see a beautiful cruise liner, surrounded by endless, beautiful blue skies and sea wouldn't that get you going? Of course it would. Images are a powerful example of how to journal and will strengthen your motivation toward your goal.

How to journal your progress toward your goals:

You can note down your thoughts, any fears, concerns and any mistakes you feel you might have made in relation to your progress toward your goals. You will gain valuable feedback on what changes you can make as well as insights into the root cause of any fears etc.,

When you're journaling such emotions, it is quite normal to feel very deeply moved. Bear in mind that the process you're working through is perfectly normal and healthy.

Think of it as you releasing emotions, which could otherwise cause you more harm if they were left unspent. View such experiences as part and parcel of the positive contributions of how to journal.

Should you encounter any adverse blocks with any of your emotions and feel the need for outside help, do consult with a qualified counselor or other practitioner.

How to journal your review:

Once you've finished recording, take a short break before reading your entry. Do be kind to yourself and avoid being critical.

After all, what you've put on paper is a valid account of **your reality**, the objective being to gain insights into how you are experiencing it and what you can now do to positively change or build on it. Now use a few lines to journal any insights, or ideas you gain from your re-read, as well as what you've learned from your writing.

While you might find your writings very revealing, equally, you might not always get such instant clarity. You may well find on occasions that you glean very little, if anything from re-reading your journals. That's fine. Just get into the practice of re-reading your entries in the coming days or even weeks.

You'll probably find that at some point, some of your insights will just seem to appear out of nowhere. You'll have found the answers within yourself and be able to return to your journal to this effect.

How to journal – Tips:

· Do keep your diary safe, private and confidential. If you harbor any fear that it is not secure or that the content might be read by other people, it could hinder your journaling by you not writing as freely as you would otherwise. Just as you'd keep your best friend's secrets close to your chest, do the same with your journal.

· Treat your journal as you would a good friend and, as your coach.

· Write a welcoming greeting or inspirational quote that is welcoming of you, each time you visit it

· Do journal anything and everything that give you cause for celebration, as well as any frustrations you experience.

Make your journal exciting and a place you will want to visit on a daily basis. As well as journaling thoughts, ideas and feelings, you can jot down inspirational quotes, short stories or anything else that will make it interesting and meaningful

The above should have answered many of your questions on how to journal as well as giving you some ideas as to the techniques you can use to do so.

Journaling is not 'set in stone'. Use a technique that best suit you, which should include your own personal style of writing. You - more than anyone else knows how to journal effectively and what's right for you.

Journaling should not be strictly reserved for when you're under stress or experiencing difficulties in your life. You'll learn just as much, if not more from journaling, when you're experiencing feelings of happiness, gratitude, joy and success. (Taken from Health Women's Healthy Living Tools).

"What lies behind us and what lies before us are tiny matters compared to what lies within us"
(Ralph Waldo Emerson)

RELAXATION AND DEEP BREATHING

About Relaxation

The ability to relax is important in effectively managing stress and anxiety. When we feel stressed, our bodies react with what is called the "fight or flight" response. Our muscles become tense, our heart and respiration rates increase, and other physiological systems become taxed. Without the ability to relax, chronic stress or anxiety can lead to burnout, anger, irritability, depression, medical problems, and more.

Allowing yourself to deeply relax is the exact opposite of the "fight or flight" response. In 1975, Herbert Benson described what he referred to as the "relaxation response." This is the body's ability to experience a decrease in heart rate, respiration rate, blood pressure, muscle tension, and oxygen consumption.

How Relaxation Exercises Can Help:

There are many benefits to being able to induce the "relaxation response" in your own body. Some benefits include a reduction of generalized anxiety, prevention of cumulative stress, increased energy, improved concentration, reduction of some physical problems, and increased self-confidence (Bourne, 2000).

Relaxation exercises can be a powerful weapon against stress. The following are some important facts about stress:

43% of adults experienced adverse health effects from stress

75-90% of visits to a physician's office are for stress-related conditions and complaints

Stress has been linked to the 6 leading causes of death: heart disease, cancer, lung ailments, accidents, cirrhosis of the liver, and suicide

The Occupational Safety and Health Administration (OSHA) have declared stress a hazard of the workplace.

In the workplace, stress may be related to lost hours due to absenteeism, reduced productivity, and worker's compensation benefits. This costs the American industry more than $300 billion annually.

Source: Miller, Smith & Rothstein, 1994

It's a Skill!

Utilizing a relaxation exercise to help reduce stress or anxiety is like learning to ride a bicycle for the first time. **It is a skill that takes time and practice to do it effectively!** We cannot expect to develop a relaxation skill after trying it one or two times, just as we cannot ride a bike well when we first try. Relaxation exercises can seem deceptively simple at first, but using them well when stress is high requires practice.

Getting the Most Out of the Online Relaxation Exercises

For each of the relaxation exercises, it is recommended that you find a nice, quiet place where you know you will not be disturbed for the duration of the exercise. Find a comfortable chair that will allow you to sit up straight using good posture. How you sit in your chair is important for maximum benefit. Push the small of your back to the rear of the chair and sit upright. This will allow you to take long smooth breaths, and your lungs to fully expand with oxygen. Do not cross your arms or legs, but sit with your legs at a ninety degree angle. Rest your arms comfortably in your lap without using armrests. If you use armrests, this might lead to muscle tension in your shoulders, neck and back.

Many people prefer to close their eyes during these relaxation exercises. If you do not wish to close your eyes, you might find a fixed point in the room and let your gaze fall upon it. Discontinue the exercise if you experience physical or emotional discomfort.

ALPHA STATE:

Ten Easy ways to achieve the best mental state for learning

Research has found that the ideal state for learning is when the brain is in a relaxed, but aware state. So when we say relaxed, we do not mean asleep. We mean relaxed, focused and aware.

At this point the brainwaves run at about 8 to 12 cycles per seconds or hertz. This is called the **alpha state**.

This compares with the 'normal' state of 13-25 hertz which is called the **beta state**. The beta state is that of most of our waking moments as we go about our daily lives.

At the other end of the spectrum we find, just below the alpha level, the **theta state** which is even slower than alpha, and an even deeper sense of relaxation.

It is however more difficult to achieve, and really requires one to have the ability to meditate deeply.

It is a highly creative state.

10 Easy Ways to achieve the Alpha State

It can be achieved in a number of ways and most of us achieve it at some during most days. A typical time may be just before one goes to sleep, or as one wakes.

At this time the mind is clear, receptive to information, and rapidly makes 'connections', realizations and joins up thoughts.

Many an 'AHA!' or 'EUREKA' moment comes at these times.

This was no doubt the state that Archimedes was in a good relaxed state when he launched himself out of the bath and down the street in his birthday suit.

The state is also great for releasing stress.

#1 Alpha Technique - Classical Superlearning Music for optimum accelerated learning

Researchers have found that certain music types ease the brainwaves into the relaxed 'alpha state' that is ideal for Superlearning. A number of sources provide such recordings which can be great for providing the background for a more effective learning session.

Has your software got it inbuilt?

One form of this superlearning music is the largo movement of certain Baroque composers. The largo movements are around 40 to 60 beats per minute.

#2 - Meditation
Meditation is a great way to get to an alpha state. There are many types of meditation methods including the famed **'Transcendental Meditation'**.

#3 Alpha Brainwaves Technique - Yoga
Certain relaxing yoga styles can be affective way to get into the relaxed optilearning state.

#4 Relaxation & Super Learning via Floatation in a Float Tank

One of the most rapid, and effective methods for getting in to an alpha state is through the use of a floatation tank. Floating has been done for centuries in the waters of places such as the Dead Sea.

But Dr Lilly who was experimenting with sensory deprivation discovered the modern floating phenomena. Rather than sending him insane, (as was the thinking at the time) floating in a dark environment led him in to a deeply relaxed, meditative state.

There are many commercial float centers worldwide where you can float for 40 to 60 minutes and drift in to a deeply relaxed state, perfect for superlearning languages, or any subject.

The float tank is like a very large bath, with a cover. Water comes up to about 50 centimeters and it has about 600 kilograms of Epsom Salts dissolved in it. The salts make the water very dense, so that whole body floats unaided, and without the need to flap or kick.

Stress just melts away, and in float tanks with speakers fitted they can be used to pipe music or learning material into while you float in a relaxed, meditative state. The physical relaxation on the body is also wonderfully de-stressing for the body.

#5 The Jose Silva Method as a tool for Superlearning

Jose Silva developed a method of dynamic meditation which is effective at getting the user in to an alpha state (find his method on the internet).

#6 Relaxation through Breathing

Rhythmic breathing in a relaxed posture and a peaceful environment is important for getting to the alpha state.

Rhythmic breathing techniques are taught by many eastern relaxation disciplines. Yoga, aikido, tai-chi to name a few.

Language learning is enhanced when students are 'fed' new information in regularly timed 'shots' of information.

In this mode, words and 'Memory Triggers' and sent out in timed bursts during which the student is prompted to breathe in, hold the breathe, and then breathe out.

The breathing prompts clear the mind, and allow the student to focus and concentrate on the material being learned.

#7 Rapid-Alpha using Light and Sound Machines - Brainwave Synchronizers

In the 1930's scientists found that strobes tend to cause brainwaves to follow the frequency pattern of the light. They also found that brainwaves follow the pulse of rhythmic sound.

For centuries man has beaten drums around the fireplace to achieve a deeply meditative, hypnotic trance-like state... so there's nothing new there!

Technology has enabled us to harness the two at accurate pulse-rates to effortlessly achieve **brainwave synchronization.**

How do Brainwave Synchronizers work?

There are a number of **light and sound machines** available which help one get to an alpha state.

Most have a thing that looks like a pair of large sunglasses into which lights are flashed at different frequencies. Different colored light bulbs allow the machine to vary the colors and patterns can be varied by varying the inputs between the left and right eye.

You lie on a bed with the 'glasses' on and close your eyes. Switch on for 'instant meditation'.

At the same time you can put on a headset through which rhythmic sounds are sent. The combination puts you into a deeply relaxed state, providing of course you have chosen such a setting.

The Headphones part of Brainwave Synchronizers

Researchers have found that if you put regularly pulsing sound at the one frequency in one ear, and sound at another frequency in the other ear, your brain will pulse at a frequency equal to the difference between the two frequencies.

...so if you put sound of 100 cycles per second (hertz) in the left ear and 110 hertz in the right ear, your brainwaves will pulse at 10 hertz .... ALPHA!

Of course by combining light and sound, at selected frequency you will understand how easily and effortlessly you can achieve the alpha state with a Brainwave Synchronizer.

#8 Alpha Technique - Biofeedback

Biofeedback is a system of training one's body to respond to various mental commands. There are now a number of machines that can help you with this.

#9 - Autogenics

Another form of biofeedback.

#10 - Alpha Technique - Before sleep

One naturally enters the alpha state as one falls asleep, and when one **slowly and naturally** wakes up. The blast of the alarm clock will shatter through theta-delta-alpha and to beta.

How does one harness this 'alpha state' on waking. Simple.

- As you awaken, just lie there and consciously direct your thoughts to the learning material you are covering, or the topics that you need to address.

  This is particularly easy when you have no pressure to get out of bed, say on a weekend.

- Use a non-alarm type alarm clock. Use one of those that just wakes you up gently, for example like with quiet music that very slowly builds up. (information from www.allaboutdepression.com).

<u>Your Choice!</u>

You may have some of your own ideas on ways to accomplish the breaking of your addiction. Find what works for you – it may be a combination of exercises, or it may be only one. But whatever you do, find one that works and work it.

Emotional Addiction keeps us in relationships that are harmful to us, hurtful to us, and focused on someone else's needs and not our own. Don't forget that for recovery, the journey is one of looking inward, focusing on self, working on personal weakness and making the changes necessary for recovery.

"Anything the mind of man can conceive – believing, it can achieve". Napoleon Hill.

References

1.Benson, H. *The Relaxation Response.* New York, NY: Morrow, 1975.

2.Bourne, E. *The Anxiety and Phobia Workbook.* 3rd. Edition. Oakland, CA: New Harbinger Publications, Inc., 2000.

3. Miller, L., and Smith, A. D., Rothstein, L. *The Stress Solution: An Action Plan to Manage the Stress in Your Life.* New York, NY: Pocket Books, 1994.

4. HealthWomensHealthyLivingandgoals.com

5. www.allaboutdepression.com

6. 200wordsaday.com

Made in the USA
Charleston, SC
04 August 2010